Good Housekeeping

Best Ever Cakes & Bakes

COLLINS & BROWN

Recipes

30-minute Fruit Cake

Shopping list

- 125g (4oz) unsalted butter, softened
- 125g (4oz) light muscovado sugar
- grated zest of 1 lemon
- 2 medium eggs
- a few drops of vanilla extract

Serves 18

Preparation Time
15 minutes

Cooking Time
30 minutes,
plus cooling

- 150g (5oz) self-raising flour, sifted
- 1 tsp baking powder
- a little lemon juice, as needed
- 50g (2oz) glacé cherries, chopped
- 175g (6oz) mixed dried fruit
- 25g (1oz) desiccated coconut
- 25g (1oz) demerara sugar
- 50g (2oz) flaked almonds

How to cook

1 Preheat the oven to 190°C (170°C fan oven) mark 5. Grease and baseline a 28 x 18cm (11 x 7in) shallow baking tin.

2 Beat together the butter, muscovado sugar, lemon zest, eggs, vanilla extract, flour and baking powder. Add a little lemon juice, if necessary, to form a soft dropping consistency. Stir in the cherries, dried fruit and coconut.

3 Spoon the mixture into the prepared tin, level the surface and sprinkle with demerara sugar and almonds. Bake for 30 minutes or until golden.

4 Cool in the tin for a few minutes, then turn out on to a wire rack to cool completely.

Orange Syrup Cake

Shopping list

- 175g (6oz) butter, plus extra to grease
- 225g (8oz) caster sugar
- 2 medium eggs, beaten
- 200g (7oz) rice flour

Serves 10

Preparation Time
20 minutes, plus soaking

Cooking Time
30–40 minutes

- 2 tsp baking powder
- 75g (3oz) ground almonds
- grated zest and juice of 1 large orange
- 250ml carton orange juice
- 2 tbsp lemon juice
- 2 large oranges, peeled and thickly sliced
- blueberries to serve

How to cook

1. Preheat the oven to 190°C (170°C fan oven) mark 5. Grease and baseline a shallow 20cm (8in) round tin.

2. Cream the butter and 75g (3oz) sugar, then beat in the eggs gradually. Fold in the flour, baking powder and ground almonds. Stir in the zest and juice of the orange and 8 tbsp orange juice. The mixture should be of a soft dropping consistency.

3. Bake in the oven for 40 minutes or until firm. Leave to cool in the tin for 10 minutes, then turn out on to a wire rack.

4. Just before serving, combine the remaining sugar and orange juice plus the lemon juice in a small pan. Add the orange slices, bring to the boil and cook for 1–2 minutes. Take the pan off the heat and leave to cool for 5 minutes. Remove the orange slices from the syrup and set aside.

5. Put the cake on a serving plate and, with a cocktail stick, prick the cake in a number of places. Drizzle with the syrup and leave to soak for 30 minutes. Serve with the orange slices and blueberries.

Sticky Ginger Ring

Shopping list

- [ ] 100g (3½oz) unsalted butter, diced, plus extra to grease
- [ ] 100g (3½oz) soft brown sugar
- [ ] 3 tbsp black treacle
- [ ] 100ml (3½fl oz) milk
- [ ] 2 tbsp brandy
- [ ] 1 large egg, beaten

Serves 8

Preparation Time
15 minutes, plus cooling

Cooking Time
1 hour

- 150g (5oz) plain flour
- 2 tsp ground ginger
- 2 tsp ground cinnamon
- 1 tsp bicarbonate of soda
- 75g (3oz) ready-to-eat pitted prunes, chopped coarsely

For the topping

- 225g (8oz) golden icing sugar, sifted
- 2 pieces preserved stem ginger, drained and roughly chopped

How to cook

1. Preheat the oven to 150°C (130°C fan oven) mark 2. Generously grease a 20.5cm (8in), 600ml (1 pint) capacity round ring mould. Put the butter, brown sugar and treacle into a pan and heat gently until melted, stirring all the time. Add the milk and brandy. Cool, then beat in the egg.

2. Sift the flour, spices and bicarbonate of soda into a large mixing bowl. Make a well in the centre, pour in the treacle mixture and stir together until all the flour has been combined – it should have a soft dropping consistency. Stir in the chopped prunes.

3. Pour the mixture into the greased mould and bake for 1 hour or until firm to the touch and a skewer inserted in the centre comes out clean. Leave in the tin for 10 minutes, then turn out on to a wire rack.

4. To make the topping, mix the icing sugar with about 2 tbsp hot water to create a coating consistency. Drizzle over the cake, then decorate with stem ginger.

Lemon & Berry Crunch Cake

Shopping list

- [ ] 150g (5oz) unsalted butter, softened, plus extra to grease
- [ ] 2 medium eggs, plus 1 egg yolk
- [ ] a pinch of salt
- [ ] 150g (5oz) caster sugar
- [ ] 150g (5oz) self-raising flour, sifted

Serves 8

Preparation Time
40 minutes,
plus setting

Cooking Time
1 hour,
plus cooling

- grated zest and juice of 1 lemon
- 125g (4oz) raspberries and blueberries

For the lemon crunch topping

- 25ml (1fl oz) bottled lemon juice
- 225g (8oz) caster sugar
- 25g (1oz) rough white sugar cubes, lightly crushed
- white currants, blackcurrants and wild strawberries, and crème fraîche or Greek yogurt to serve

How to cook

1 Preheat the oven to 170°C (150°C fan oven) mark 3. Grease and baseline a 1.1 litre (2 pint) loaf tin.

2 Lightly beat the eggs and egg yolk with the salt. Put the butter and sugar into a bowl and beat until light and fluffy. Gradually beat in the eggs, beating for about 10 minutes.

3 Fold in the flour with the lemon zest and 2 tbsp of the juice (put the rest to one side). Fold in the raspberries and blueberries. Spoon the mixture into the prepared tin and bake for 50 minutes–1 hour. Leave in the tin for 5 minutes, then turn out on to a wire rack to cool.

4 To make the topping, mix together the reserved fresh lemon juice, the bottled lemon juice and caster sugar. Spoon over the cake and sprinkle the top with crushed sugar. Set aside for 1 hour. Slice and serve with the berries and the crème fraîche or yogurt.

Raspberry & Peach Cake

Shopping list

- 200g (7oz) unsalted butter, melted, plus extra to grease
- 250g (9oz) self-raising flour, sifted
- 100g (3½oz) golden caster sugar
- 4 medium eggs, beaten

Serves 8

Preparation Time
15 minutes

Cooking Time
1–1¼ hours, plus cooling

- 125g (4oz) raspberries
- 2 large almost-ripe peaches or nectarines, halved, stoned and sliced
- 4 tbsp apricot jam
- juice of ½ lemon

How to cook

1. Preheat the oven to 190°C (170°C fan oven) mark 5. Grease a 20.5cm (8in) springform cake tin and baseline with baking parchment.

2. Put the flour and sugar into a large bowl. Make a well in the centre and add the melted butter and the eggs. Mix well.

3. Spread half the mixture over the base of the cake tin and add half the raspberries and peaches or nectarines. Spoon on the remaining cake mixture, smooth over, then add the remaining raspberries and peaches or nectarines, pressing them down into the mixture slightly.

4. Bake for 1–1¼ hours until risen and golden, and a skewer inserted into the centre comes out clean. Remove from the oven and leave in the tin to cool for 10 minutes.

5. Warm the jam and lemon juice together in a small pan and brush over the cake to glaze.

Apple & Blueberry Cake

Shopping list

- 125g (4oz) unsalted butter, diced, plus extra to grease
- 225g (8oz) self-raising flour, sifted
- ½ tsp salt
- 175g (6oz) granulated sugar, golden if possible
- 2 large eggs, beaten

Serves 8

Preparation Time
20 minutes, plus cooling

Cooking Time
1 hour, plus cooling

- 2 large Granny Smith apples, peeled, cored and sliced
- 150g (5oz) blueberries
- 175g (6oz) apricot jam
- 1 tbsp lemon juice

How to cook

1 Preheat the oven to 190°C (170°C fan oven) mark 5. Grease and baseline a 20.5cm (8in) springform tin with non-stick baking parchment. Put the flour and salt into a large mixing bowl, add the diced butter and rub in the flour until the mixture looks like fine breadcrumbs. Add 150g (5oz) sugar with the beaten eggs and stir well.

2 Spread half the mixture in a thin layer in the tin, then layer the sliced apples and the blueberries evenly over the surface, setting aside a little of the fruit for the top of the cake. Sprinkle with the remaining sugar, then spoon in the rest of the cake mixture. Add the remaining apple slices and blueberries, pressing them down slightly into the mixture.

3 Bake for 45–55 minutes until risen and firm to the touch – a skewer inserted into the centre of the cake should come out clean. Cool in the tin for 10 minutes, then turn out on to a wire rack to cool.

4 Warm the jam and lemon juice in a small pan until evenly combined. Sieve the mixture and, while it's still warm, brush it over the top of the cake. Serve immediately.

Warm Lemon Syrup Cake

Shopping list

- 225g (8oz) unsalted butter, softened, plus extra to grease
- grated zest of 2 lemons and 2 tbsp lemon juice
- 225g (8oz) caster sugar
- 4 large eggs, beaten
- 225g (8oz) self-raising flour, sifted
- 75g (3oz) candied lemon peel, finely chopped (optional)

Serves 12

Preparation Time
15 minutes

Cooking Time
1 hour,
plus cooling

For the syrup and topping

- 175g (6oz) caster sugar
- finely sliced zest and strained juice of 3 lemons
- 75ml (3fl oz) water

How to cook

1. Preheat the oven to 180°C (160°C fan oven) mark 4. Grease and baseline a 20.5cm (8in) round deep cake tin.

2. Cream together the butter and lemon zest. Gradually beat in the sugar, followed by the eggs; the mixture should be stiff. Fold in the flour, candied peel, if using, and lemon juice. Spoon the mixture into the prepared tin and bake for about 1 hour or until golden.

3. Meanwhile, prepare the syrup and topping. Put the sugar, lemon juice and water into a pan. Warm gently until the sugar dissolves, then bring to the boil and bubble for 1 minute. Cool.

4. As soon as the cake is cooked, turn out into a shallow dish and immediately spoon over the syrup. Leave for about 30 minutes for the syrup to soak in. Serve warm, topped with the sliced lemon zest.

Gluten-free Chocolate Cake

Shopping list

- 125g (4oz) butter, softened, plus extra to grease
- 200g (7oz) light muscovado sugar
- 2 large eggs, lightly beaten
- 125g (4oz) gluten-free plain chocolate, broken into pieces, melted and left to cool slightly
- 100g (3½oz) natural yogurt

Serves 10

Preparation Time
30 minutes

Cooking Time
45 minutes – 1 hour, plus cooling

- few drops of vanilla extract
- 200g (7oz) brown rice flour
- ½ tsp wheat-free baking powder
- 1 tsp bicarbonate of soda

For the icing

- 150g (5oz) gluten-free plain chocolate, broken into pieces
- 150ml (¼ pint) double cream
- large milk and plain or white chocolate buttons (gluten-free) to decorate

How to cook

1 Preheat the oven to 180°C (160°C fan oven) mark 4. Grease a deep 18cm (7in) square cake tin and line with greaseproof paper.

2 Cream the butter and sugar together until light and fluffy. Gradually beat in the eggs, then the melted chocolate, yogurt and vanilla extract. Sift together the rice flour, baking powder and bicarbonate of soda. Beat into the mixture a little at a time. Pour into the prepared tin and bake for 45 minutes–1 hour or until a skewer inserted in the centre comes out clean. Leave to cool in the tin for 10 minutes, then transfer to a wire rack to cool completely.

3 To make the icing, put the chocolate into a heatproof bowl. Heat the cream to just below boiling point. Pour on to the chocolate. Leave for 5 minutes, then beat until the chocolate has melted and the mixture is smooth. Cool until thickened, then spread all over the cake with a palette knife. Decorate the top and sides with alternate milk and plain or white chocolate buttons to create a polka-dot effect.

White Chocolate Mousse Cake

Shopping list

- vegetable oil to grease
- 450g (1lb) white chocolate
- 285ml (9½fl oz) double cream

Serves 10

Preparation Time
30 minutes, plus overnight freezing

Cooking Time
20–30 minutes

- finely grated zest of 1 large orange
- 2 tsp orange liqueur, such as Grand Marnier
- 300ml (½ pint) full-fat Greek yogurt

How to cook

1. Lightly oil a shallow 20cm (8in) round cake tin and line with baking parchment.
2. Break the chocolate into pieces and put into a large bowl with half the cream. Bring a large pan of water to the boil, remove from the heat and sit the bowl of chocolate and cream on top, making sure the base of the bowl doesn't touch the water. Leave for 20–30 minutes until the chocolate has melted. Don't stir; just leave it to melt.
3. Meanwhile, put the orange zest and liqueur into a small bowl. Set aside to soak. Whip the remaining cream until it just holds its shape.
4. Remove the bowl of melted chocolate from the pan and beat in the yogurt. Fold in the cream with the zest and liqueur mix.
5. Spoon the mixture into the prepared tin, cover with clingfilm and freeze overnight or for up to one month. One hour before serving, transfer from the freezer to the refrigerator. Unwrap and put on a serving plate.

Chocolate Butterfly Cakes

Shopping list

- 125g (4oz) very soft butter
- 125g (4oz) caster sugar
- 2 medium eggs, lightly beaten individually
- 125g (4oz) plain flour

Serves 18

Preparation Time
25 minutes

Cooking Time
15–20 minutes, plus cooling

- 25g (1oz) cocoa
- ½ tsp baking powder
- 1 tbsp milk
- buttercream icing (see Cook's Tips)

For the buttercream

- 75g (3oz) unsalted butter
- 175g (6oz) icing sugar, sifted
- a few drops of vanilla extract
- 1–2 tbsp milk

How to cook

1. Preheat the oven to 190°C (170°C fan oven) mark 5. Put 18 paper cake cases into two bun trays. With an electric hand whisk, beat the butter and sugar together until soft and fluffy and lighter in colour. Beat in the eggs thoroughly, one at a time.

2. Sift the flour, cocoa and baking powder into the bowl and fold in gently until well mixed. Fold in the milk to give a soft, dropping consistency.

3. Divide the mixture between the cases and bake for 15–20 minutes until firm. Cool on a wire rack.

4. To make the buttercream, soften the butter in a mixing bowl, then beat until light and fluffy. Gradually stir in the remaining ingredients and beat until smooth. Allow the icing to settle before using.

5. Slice off the top of each cake and cut the slice in half. Spread buttercream on each cake with a palette knife. Put the 'butterfly wings' on top, with their curved sides facing each other.

Blackberry & Cinnamon Loaf

Shopping list

- 125ml (4fl oz) sunflower oil, plus extra to grease
- 175g (6oz) plain flour
- 1½ tsp baking powder
- 1½ tsp ground cinnamon
- 200g (7oz) frozen blackberries

Serves 8

Preparation Time
15 minutes

Cooking Time
55 minutes, plus cooling

- 125g (4oz) golden caster sugar
- grated zest and juice of 1 lemon
- 125ml (4fl oz) Greek yogurt
- 3 medium eggs, beaten
- icing sugar to dust

How to cook

1. Preheat the oven to 190°C (170°C fan oven) mark 5. Grease and baseline a 900g (2lb) loaf tin.

2. Sift the flour, baking powder and cinnamon into a bowl, add the frozen berries and toss to coat. Make a well in the centre.

3. In another bowl, whisk together the caster sugar, oil, lemon zest and juice, yogurt and eggs. Pour into the well in the flour mixture and stir.

4. Spoon the mixture into the prepared tin, level the surface and bake for 55 minutes (cover lightly with foil if the top is browning too quickly) or until a skewer inserted into the centre comes out clean. Leave in the tin to cool. Remove from the tin and dust with icing sugar.

Cook's Tip

Apple and Cinnamon Yogurt Loaf: replace the blackberries with 2 small Cox's or Braeburn apples, peeled, cored and chopped.

Banana & Chocolate Loaf

Shopping list

- butter to grease
- 175g (6oz) plain flour, sifted
- 2 tsp baking powder
- ½ tsp bicarbonate of soda
- ½ tsp salt

Serves 15

Preparation Time
20 minutes

Cooking Time
1 hour,
plus cooling

- 175g (6oz) light muscovado sugar
- 2 large eggs
- 3 medium ripe bananas, mashed
- 150g (5oz) natural yogurt
- 150g (5oz) butterscotch chocolate or milk chocolate, roughly chopped
- 100g (3½oz) pecan nuts, chopped
- 1–2 tbsp demerara sugar

How to cook

1 Preheat the oven to 170°C (150°C fan oven) mark 3. Grease and line a 1.4kg (3lb) loaf tin.

2 Put the flour, baking powder, bicarbonate of soda and salt into a large bowl and mix together.

3 In a separate bowl, beat together the muscovado sugar and eggs with an electric hand whisk until pale and fluffy. Carefully stir in the bananas, yogurt, chocolate and 50g (2oz) pecan nuts, followed by the flour mixture.

4 Spoon the mixture into the prepared tin and sprinkle the remaining chopped pecan nuts and the demerara sugar over. Bake for 1 hour or until a skewer inserted into the centre comes out clean. Leave to cool in the tin, then turn out and slice.

Ultimate Chocolate Brownie

Shopping list

- 200g (7oz) butter, plus extra to grease
- 400g (14oz) plain chocolate
- 225g (8oz) light muscovado sugar
- 1 tsp vanilla extract

Serves 16

Preparation Time
15 minutes

Cooking Time
1 hour 20 minutes, plus cooling

- 150g (5oz) pecan nuts, roughly chopped
- 25g (1oz) cocoa powder, sifted, plus extra to dust (optional)
- 75g (3oz) self-raising flour, sifted
- 3 large eggs, beaten

How to cook

1 Preheat the oven to 170°C (150°C fan oven) mark 3. Grease a 20.5cm (8in) square shallow cake tin and line the base with non-stick baking parchment. Put the butter and chocolate into a heatproof bowl over a pan of gently simmering water and stir until melted. Remove from the heat and stir in the sugar, vanilla extract, pecan nuts, cocoa, flour and eggs.

2 Turn the mixture into the prepared tin and level the surface with the back of a spoon. Bake for about 1 hour 15 minutes or until set on the surface but still soft underneath.

3 Leave to cool in the tin for 2 hours. Turn out, dust with sifted cocoa powder, if using, and cut into squares. Eat cold or serve warm with ice cream.

Cook's Tip

The secret to really moist, squidgy brownies is all in the timing. A few minutes too long in the oven will produce a dry texture, so be careful not to over-bake them.

Chocolate Cup Cakes

Shopping list

- 125g (4oz) unsalted butter, softened
- 125g (4oz) light muscovado sugar
- 2 medium eggs, beaten
- 15g (½oz) cocoa powder

Makes 18

Preparation Time
15 minutes

Cooking Time
20 minutes, plus cooling and setting

- 100g (3½oz) self-raising flour
- 100g (3½oz) plain chocolate (at least 70% cocoa solids), roughly chopped

For the topping

- 150ml (¼ pint) double cream
- 100g (3½oz) plain chocolate (at least 70% cocoa solids), broken up

How to cook

1. Preheat the oven to 190°C (170°C fan oven) mark 5. Line bun tins or muffin pans with 18 paper muffin cases.
2. Beat together the butter and sugar until light and fluffy. Gradually beat in the eggs. Sift the cocoa powder with the flour and fold into the creamed mixture with the chopped chocolate.
3. Divide the mixture among the paper cases and lightly flatten the surface with the back of a spoon. Bake for 20 minutes. Cool in the cases.
4. For the topping, put the cream and broken-up chocolate into a heavy-based pan over a low heat and heat until melted, then allow to cool and thicken slightly. Pour over the cooled cakes and leave to set for 30 minutes.

Fairy Cakes

Shopping list

- 125g (4oz) self-raising flour, sifted
- 1 tsp baking powder
- 125g (4oz) caster sugar
- 125g (4oz) very soft butter
- 2 medium eggs

Serves 18

Preparation Time
20 minutes

Cooking Time
10–15 minutes, plus cooling

- I tbsp milk
- 225g (8oz) icing sugar, sifted
- assorted food colourings (optional)
- sweets, sprinkles or coloured sugar to decorate

How to cook

1. Preheat the oven to 200°C (180°C fan oven) mark 6. Put paper cases into 18 of the holes in two bun tins. Put the flour, baking powder, sugar, butter, eggs and milk into a mixing bowl and beat with an electric hand whisk for 2 minutes until the mixture is pale and very soft.

2. Half-fill each paper case with the mixture. Bake for 10–15 minutes until golden brown. Transfer to a wire rack to cool.

3. Put the icing sugar into a bowl and gradually blend in 2–3 tbsp warm water until the icing is fairly stiff, but spreadable. Add a couple of drops of food colouring, if you like. When the cakes are cold, spread the tops with the icing and decorate.

Apple Madeleines

Shopping list

- 150g (5oz) unsalted butter, melted and cooled, plus extra to grease
- 3 large eggs
- 150g (5oz) caster sugar
- 1 tsp vanilla extract

Makes 24

Preparation Time
15 minutes

Cooking Time
8 – 10 minutes, plus cooling

- 150g (5oz) plain flour, sifted
- ½ tsp baking powder
- 2 apples such as Cox's, peeled, cored and finely chopped
- icing sugar to dust

How to cook

1 Preheat the oven to 200°C (180°C fan oven) mark 6. Grease the madeleine tins.

2 Using an electric whisk, beat the eggs and caster sugar together until pale and thick (this should take about 8 minutes), then add the vanilla extract. Quickly but gently, fold in the flour, baking powder and apples followed by the melted butter, making sure the butter doesn't settle at the bottom of the bowl.

3 Spoon the mixture into the madeleine tins. Bake for 8–10 minutes until golden, then remove from the tins and cool on a wire rack. Store in an airtight container for up to two days. Dust with icing sugar before serving.

Cook's Tip

Lemon Madeleines: omit the vanilla extract and apples. Stir 2 tbsp clear honey into the warm melted butter, then leave to cool. Add the grated zest of 1 lemon together with the flour.

Kitten Cup Cakes

Shopping list

- 125g (4oz) very soft butter
- 125g (4oz) caster sugar
- grated zest of 1 lemon
- 2 medium eggs, beaten
- 125g (4oz) self-raising flour, sifted

Makes 12

Preparation Time
25 minutes

Cooking Time
20 minutes, plus cooling

For the decoration

- 175g (6oz) icing sugar
- black and assorted writing icings
- jelly diamonds and Smarties
- black liquorice laces, cut into short lengths

How to cook

1. Preheat the oven to 190°C (170°C fan oven) mark 5. Put paper cases into a 12-hole bun tin.

2. Beat the butter, caster sugar and lemon zest together with an electric hand whisk until pale and fluffy. Add the eggs, a little at a time, beating well after each addition. Fold in the flour. Divide the mixture between the paper cases. Bake for about 20 minutes until golden and risen. Cool on a wire rack.

3. Sift the icing sugar into a bowl. Stir in 1–2 tbsp warm water, a few drops at a time, until you have a smooth, spreadable icing. Slice the tops off the cooled buns to make them level, if necessary. Cover the top of each cake with icing.

4. Decorate the buns to make kittens' faces. Use black writing icing for the eyes, halve the jelly diamonds for the ears, press a Smartie in the centre for a nose, and use black writing icing to draw on a mouth. Use different coloured writing icing for the pupils and markings. Stick on liquorice whiskers.

Vanilla Cup Cakes

Shopping list

- 125g (4oz) softened butter
- 125g (4oz) golden caster sugar
- 2 medium eggs

Makes 12

Preparation Time
5 minutes

Cooking Time
15 – 20 minutes

- 125g (4oz) self-raising flour
- 1 tbsp vanilla extract
- 200g (7oz) white chocolate

How to cook

1. Preheat the oven to 190°C (170°C fan oven) mark 5. Line a bun tin or muffin pan with 12 paper cases.

2. Beat the butter, sugar, eggs, flour and vanilla until smooth and creamy. Half-fill the muffin cases with the mixture and bake for 15–20 minutes until pale golden, risen and springy to the touch. Transfer to a wire rack to cool.

3. When the cupcakes are cool, melt the chocolate (see Cook's Tip), spoon over the cakes and leave to set.

Cook's Tip

To melt chocolate, break the chocolate into pieces and put into a heatproof bowl set over a pan of gently simmering water. Heat very gently until the chocolate starts to melt, then stir regularly until completely melted.

Spiced Carrot Muffins

Shopping list

- 125g (4oz) unsalted butter, softened
- 125g (4oz) light muscovado sugar
- 3 pieces of preserved stem ginger, drained and chopped
- 150g (5oz) self-raising flour, sifted
- 1½ tsp baking powder
- 1 tbsp ground mixed spice

Makes 12

Preparation Time
30 minutes

Cooking Time
20–25 minutes, plus cooling

- 25g (1oz) ground almonds
- 3 medium eggs
- finely grated zest of ½ orange
- 150g (5oz) carrots, grated
- 50g (2oz) pecan nuts, chopped
- 50g (2oz) sultanas
- 200g (7oz) full-fat cream cheese
- 75g (3oz) icing sugar
- 1 tsp lemon juice
- 3 tbsp white rum or orange liqueur (optional)
- 12 unsprayed rose petals to decorate (optional)

How to cook

1 Preheat the oven to 180°C (160°C fan oven) mark 4. Line a bun tin or muffin pan with 12 paper muffin cases.

2 Beat together the butter, muscovado sugar and stem ginger until pale and creamy.

3 Add the flour, baking powder, spice, ground almonds, eggs and orange zest. Beat well until combined.

4 Stir in the carrots, pecan nuts and sultanas. Divide the mixture among the muffin cases and bake for 20–25 minutes until risen and just firm. A skewer inserted into the centre should come out clean. Transfer to a wire rack and leave to cool.

5 To make the icing, beat the cream cheese in a bowl until softened. Beat in the icing sugar and lemon juice to give a smooth icing that just holds its shape. Drizzle each cake with a little liqueur, if using. Use a small palette knife to spread a little icing over each cake. Decorate each with a petal, if you like.

White Chocolate Cup Cakes

Shopping list

- 125g (4oz) unsalted butter, at room temperature
- 125g (4oz) golden caster sugar
- 1 vanilla pod
- 2 medium eggs

Serves 12

Preparation Time
25 minutes

Cooking Time
15–20 minutes, plus cooling

- 125g (4oz) self-raising flour, sifted
- 1 tbsp vanilla extract
- 200g (7oz) white chocolate, in small pieces

For the frosted flowers

- 1 medium egg white
- 6 edible violets
- caster sugar to dust

How to cook

1. Preheat the oven to 190°C (170°C fan oven) mark 5. Line a bun tin with 12 paper muffin cases.

2. Put the butter and sugar into a bowl. Split the vanilla pod lengthways, scrape out the seeds and add to the bowl. Add the eggs, flour and vanilla extract and beat thoroughly, using an electric whisk, until smooth and creamy. Spoon the mixture into the muffin cases and bake for 15–20 minutes until pale golden, risen and springy to the touch. Leave in the tin for 2–3 minutes, then transfer to a wire rack to cool.

3. To make the frosted flowers, whisk the egg white in a clean bowl for 30 seconds until frothy. Brush over the violet petals and put on a wire rack. Lightly dust with caster sugar and leave to dry.

4. Melt the chocolate in a heatproof bowl set over a pan of gently simmering water. Stir until smooth and leave to cool slightly. Spoon the chocolate on to the cakes, top with a frosted flower and leave to set.

Ginger & Fruit Teabread

Shopping list

- 125g (4oz) each dried apricots, apples and stoned prunes, chopped
- 300ml (½ pint) strong fruit tea
- a little butter to grease
- 25g (1oz) stem ginger in syrup, chopped

12 slices

Preparation Time
15 minutes, plus 2 hours soaking

Cooking Time
1 hour, plus cooling

- 225g (8oz) wholemeal flour
- 2 tsp baking powder
- 125g (4oz) dark muscovado sugar
- 1 egg, beaten

How to cook

1. Put the dried fruit into a large bowl. Add the tea and leave to soak for 2 hours.

2. Preheat the oven to 180°C (160°C fan oven) mark 4. Grease and line the base of a 900g (2lb) loaf tin.

3. Add the remaining ingredients to the soaked fruit and mix thoroughly. Spoon into the prepared tin and brush with 2 tbsp cold water. Bake in the oven for 1 hour until cooked through.

4. Cool in the tin for 10–15 minutes, then turn out on to a wire rack to cool completely. Wrap in clingfilm and store in an airtight container. It will keep for up to three days.

Red Nose Cup Cakes

Shopping list

- (2oz) very soft butter
- 50g (2oz) caster sugar
- 1 medium egg, beaten
- 50g (2oz) self-raising flour
- ¼ tsp baking powder

Makes 36

Preparation Time
20 minutes

Cooking Time
12–15 minutes, plus cooling

- 1 ripe banana, peeled and mashed
- 125g (4oz) icing sugar, sifted
- about 1 tbsp orange juice
- red glacé cherries or round red jelly sweets to decorate

How to cook

1. Preheat the oven to 190°C (170°C fan oven) mark 5. Put the butter, caster sugar, egg, flour and baking powder into a food processor and process until smooth and well mixed. Add the banana and process for 1 minute.

2. Arrange about 36 petits fours cases on baking sheets. Put a teaspoonful of the mixture into each case. Bake for about 12–15 minutes until golden. Transfer to a wire rack to cool.

3. When the buns are cold, make glacé icing by mixing the icing sugar with the orange juice until smooth and just thick enough to coat the back of a spoon. Top each bun with a small blob of icing and stick half a cherry or a sweet on each one. Leave to set.

Nutty Fudge Shortbread

Shopping list

- 225g (8oz) unsalted butter, softened, plus extra to grease
- 300g (11oz) plain flour, sifted
- pinch of salt
- 125g (4oz) caster sugar
- 125g (4oz) light muscovado sugar, sifted

16 squares

Preparation Time
10 minutes, plus 3 hours chilling

Cooking Time
40 minutes, plus cooling

- 2 tbsp golden syrup
- 170g can condensed milk
- 300g (11oz) plain chocolate
- 100g (3½oz) walnut halves
- 100g (3½oz) hazelnuts, lightly toasted

How to cook

1. Preheat the oven to 180°C (160°C fan oven) mark 4. Grease a 20.5 x 30.5cm (8 x 12in) Swiss roll tin. Whiz the flour, salt, caster sugar and 150g (5oz) butter in a food processor until it begins to come together. (Alternatively, use a food mixer.) Press the mixture into the prepared tin and smooth over with the back of a spoon. Bake for 20–30 minutes until golden. Leave to cool in the tin.

2. Put the remaining butter, the muscovado sugar, golden syrup and condensed milk into a pan and heat gently but don't boil. Whisk together until combined. Pour over the shortbread, smooth the surface, cool, then chill for 3 hours.

3. Melt the chocolate in a heatproof bowl over a pan of gently simmering water. Stir in the nuts, then pour over the fudge mixture. Smooth the top and leave to set. Cut into 16 pieces to serve.

Carrot Traybake

Shopping list

- 100g (3½oz) unsalted butter, chopped, plus extra to grease
- 150g (5oz) carrots, grated
- 100g (3½oz) each sultanas and chopped dried dates
- 50g (2oz) tenderised coconut
- 1 tsp ground cinnamon and ½ tsp freshly grated nutmeg
- 330g bottle maple syrup

16 squares

Preparation Time
30 minutes, plus cooling

Cooking Time
50 minutes – 1 hour 5 minutes, plus cooling

- 150ml (¼ pint) apple juice
- grated zest and juice of 2 oranges
- 225g (8oz) wholemeal self-raising flour, sifted
- 2 tsp bicarbonate of soda
- 125g (4oz) walnut pieces

For the topping

- pared zest from ½–1 orange
- 200g (7oz) each cream cheese and crème fraîche
- 2 tbsp icing sugar
- 1 tsp vanilla extract

How to cook

1. Preheat the oven to 190°C (170°C fan oven) mark 5. Grease and line a 23cm (9in) square cake tin.

2. Put the butter, carrots, sultanas, dates, coconut, spices, maple syrup, apple juice and orange zest and juice into a large pan. Cover and bring to the boil, then cook for 5 minutes. Tip into a bowl and leave to cool.

3. Put the flour, bicarbonate of soda and walnuts into a large bowl and stir together. Add the cooled carrot mixture and stir well.

4. Spoon the mixture into the prepared tin and bake for 45 minutes–1 hour until firm. Leave in the tin for 10 minutes, then transfer to a wire rack to cool completely.

5. To make the topping, finely slice the orange zest. Put the cream cheese, crème fraîche, icing sugar and vanilla extract into a bowl and stir with a spatula until well combined. Spread evenly over the cake. Cut into 16 squares, then top with the orange zest.

Fruit & Nut Flapjack Bites

Shopping list

- 250g (9oz) unsalted butter, cut into pieces, plus extra to grease
- 250g (9oz) caster sugar
- 175g (6oz) golden syrup

36 squares

Preparation Time
10 minutes

Cooking Time
25 – 30 minutes, plus cooling

- 425g (15oz) rolled oats
- 125g (4oz) mixed dried fruit, including glacé cherries
- 75g (3oz) chopped nuts, toasted

How to cook

1. Preheat the oven to 180°C (160°C fan oven) mark 4. Grease a shallow 28 x 20.5cm (11 x 8in) baking tin.

2. Put the butter, sugar and syrup into a large, heavy-based pan. Stir over a moderate heat until the butter has melted. Remove from the heat and stir in the oats, dried fruit and nuts.

3. Turn into the prepared tin and level the surface. Bake for 25–30 minutes until deep golden around the edges; the mixture will still be very soft in the middle. Leave in the tin until almost cold. Remove from the tin and cut into squares. Store in an airtight tin. It will keep for up to a week.

Cook's Tip

Don't worry if your baking tin is not the exact size; use one of similar dimensions.

Sour Cherry Cup Cakes

Shopping list

- 175g (6oz) unsalted butter, softened
- 175g (6oz) golden caster sugar
- 3 medium eggs
- 175g (6oz) self-raising flour, sifted

Makes 12

Preparation Time
30 minutes

Cooking Time
15 – 20 minutes, plus cooling

- 75g (3oz) dried cherries
- 2 tbsp milk
- 225g (8oz) golden icing sugar, sifted
- 3 tbsp lemon juice, strained

How to cook

1. Preheat the oven to 190°C (170°C fan oven) mark 5. Line a bun tin or muffin pan with 12 paper muffin cases.

2. Put the butter and caster sugar into a bowl and cream together until pale, light and fluffy. Beat in the eggs, one at a time, folding in 1 tbsp flour if the mixture looks like it is starting to curdle.

3. Put 12 dried cherries to one side. Fold the remaining flour, cherries and the milk into the creamed mixture until evenly combined. Spoon the mixture into the paper cases and bake for 15–20 minutes until pale golden and risen. Remove from the tin and cool on a wire rack.

4. Put the icing sugar into a bowl and mix with the lemon juice to make a smooth dropping consistency. Spoon on to the cakes and decorate each with a cherry.

Quick Chocolate Slices

Shopping list

- 225g (8oz) butter or olive oil spread
- 50g (2oz) cocoa, sifted
- 3 tbsp golden syrup

40 fingers

Preparation Time
10 minutes

Cooking Time
2 minutes

- 300g pack digestive biscuits, crushed
- 400g (14oz) plain chocolate (at least 70 per cent cocoa solids), broken into pieces

How to cook

1. Put the butter or olive oil spread into a heatproof bowl, add the cocoa and golden syrup and melt over a pan of gently simmering water. Mix everything together.

2. Remove from the heat and stir in the biscuits. Mix well until thoroughly coated in chocolate, crushing down any large pieces of biscuit. Turn into a greased 25.5 x 16.5cm (10 x 6½in) tin. Cool, cover and chill for 20 minutes.

3. Melt the chocolate in a heatproof bowl in a 900W microwave on full power for 1 minute 40 seconds, stirring twice. Alternatively, melt over a pan of gently simmering water. Stir once more and pour over the chocolate biscuit base, then chill for 20 minutes.

4. Cut in half lengthways. Cut each half into 20 rectangular fingers.

Cook's Tip

Buy chocolate from the baking aisle – it's often cheaper than the well-known brands.

Dainty Cup Cakes

Shopping list

- 175g (6oz) unsalted butter, softened
- 175g (6oz) golden caster sugar
- 3 medium eggs
- 175g (6oz) self-raising flour, sifted
- finely grated zest and juice of 1 lemon

Makes 12

Preparation Time
15 minutes

Cooking Time
15–20 minutes, plus cooling

For the frosted flowers

- 1 medium egg white
- 6 edible flowers, such as violas
- caster sugar to dust

For the icing

- 225g (8oz) icing sugar, sifted
- 1 drop violet food colouring
- 2–3 tbsp lemon juice, strained

How to cook

1 Preheat the oven to 190°C (170°C fan oven) mark 5. Line a bun tin or muffin pan with 12 paper muffin cases.

2 Put the butter and caster sugar into a bowl and cream together until pale, light and fluffy. Add the eggs, one at a time, and beat together, folding 1 tbsp flour into the mixture if it looks as if it is going to curdle. Fold in the flour, lemon zest and juice and mix everything well.

3 Spoon the mixture into the cases and bake for 15–20 minutes until pale golden, risen and springy to the touch. Cool on a wire rack.

4 To make the frosted flowers, whisk the egg white in a clean bowl for 30 seconds until frothy. Brush over the flower petals and put on a wire rack resting on a piece of greaseproof paper. Dust heavily with caster sugar, then leave the flowers to dry.

5 To make the icing, put the icing sugar into a bowl with the violet food colouring. Mix in the lemon juice to make a smooth dropping consistency. Spoon the icing on to the cakes. Decorate with the frosted flowers and leave until the icing is set.

Almond Cookies

Shopping list

- rice paper to line
- 2 medium egg whites
- 200g (7oz) caster sugar
- 200g (7oz) ground almonds
- finely grated zest of I orange

Makes 12

Preparation Time
15 minutes

Cooking Time
15–20 minutes, plus cooling

- ½ tsp ground ginger
- 40g (1½oz) stem ginger in syrup, drained and roughly chopped
- 2 tbsp plain flour, sifted, to dust
- 12 natural glacé cherries

How to cook

1. Preheat the oven to 180°C (160°C fan oven) mark 4. Line two baking sheets with rice paper. Put the egg whites into a large bowl and whisk until they form stiff peaks. In another large bowl, stir together the sugar, ground almonds, orange zest, ¼ tsp ground ginger and the stem ginger. With a wooden spoon, mix in the egg whites to form a sticky dough.

2. Roll the dough into 12 equal-sized balls. Mix together the flour and the remaining ground ginger in a bowl. Lightly coat each ball in the flour and shake off the excess. Put the balls, spaced well apart, on to the prepared baking sheets. Flatten each one into rounds.

3. Push a glacé cherry in the middle of each cookie and bake for 15–20 minutes until lightly golden.

4. Cool on a wire rack, then trim away the excess rice paper. Store in an airtight container for up to one week.

Peanut & Raisin Cookies

Shopping list

- 125g (4oz) unsalted butter, softened, plus extra to grease
- 150g (5oz) caster sugar
- 1 medium egg
- 150g (5oz) plain flour, sifted

Makes 30

Preparation Time
10 minutes

Cooking Time
15 minutes, plus cooling

- ½ tsp baking powder
- ½ tsp salt
- 125g (4oz) crunchy peanut butter
- 175g (6oz) raisins

How to cook

1. Preheat the oven to 190°C (170°C fan oven) mark 5 and grease two baking sheets. Beat together all the ingredients except the raisins, until well blended. Stir in the raisins.

2. Spoon large teaspoonfuls of the mixture on to the baking sheets, leaving room for the mixture to spread. Bake for about 15 minutes or until golden brown around the edges.

3. Leave to cool slightly, then transfer to a wire rack to cool completely.

Cook's Tip

Chocolate Nut Cookies: omit the peanut butter and raisins and add 1 tsp vanilla extract. Stir in 175g (6oz) roughly chopped chocolate and 75g (3oz) roughly chopped walnuts.

Coconut and Cherry Cookies: omit the peanut butter and raisins, reduce the sugar to 75g (3oz) and stir in 50g (2oz) desiccated coconut and 125g (4oz) rinsed, roughly chopped glacé cherries.

The Good Housekeeping Easy to Make! series features the following bestselling titles:

One Pot
ISBN 978-1-84340-447-7

Family Meals in Minutes
ISBN 978-1-84340-495-8

Cooking for Friends
ISBN 978-1-84340-551-1

Chicken
ISBN 978-1-84340-497-2

Wok & Stir Fry
ISBN 978-1-84340-465-1

Speedy Meals
ISBN 978-1-84340-448-4

Pasta, Rice & Noodles
ISBN 978-1-84340-499-6

BBQs & Grills
ISBN 978-1-84340-449-1

Cakes & Bakes
ISBN 978-1-84340-441-5

Chocolate
ISBN 978-1-84340-494-1

Christmas
ISBN 978-1-84340-463-7

Favourite Family Meals
ISBN 978-1-84340-439-2

Feel Good Meals
ISBN 978-1-84340-440-8

Hot & Spicy
ISBN 978-184340-501-6

Kids' Cakes & Party Food
ISBN 978-184340-500-9

Low GI
ISBN 978-1-84340-466-8

First published in Great Britain in 2010
by Collins & Brown
10 Southcombe Street
London W14 0RA

An imprint of Anova Books Company Ltd
www.anovabooks.com

The Good Housekeeping website is:
www.allaboutyou.com/goodhousekeeping

ISBN 978-1-84340-586-3

The recipes in this book have been chosen from titles in the Good Housekeeping Easy to Make! series.

A catalogue record for this book is available from the British Library.

Reproduction by Dot Gradations Ltd, UK
Printed and bound by Graphicom, Italy

Photographers: Nicki Dowey; Lucinda Symons (page 6); Will Heap (page 44); Neil Barclay (page 56).